WHO'S IN CHARGE HERE? 1992

Gerald Gardner

WINGS BOOKS
New York · Avenel, New Jersey

For Terre and Marvin Hamlisch.

Photos courtesy of Reuters/Bettmann,
Wide World Photos, The White House,
Tri-Star Pictures, Columbia Pictures,
and Paramount Pictures.

Copyright © 1992 by Gerald Gardner

Published by Wings Books,
distributed by Outlet Book Company, Inc.,
a Random House Company,
40 Engelhard Avenue,
Avenel, New Jersey 07001.

Printed and Bound in the United States of America.

Cover design by Melissa Ring

Library of Congress Cataloging-in-Publication Data
Gardner, Gerald C.
Who's in charge here? : 1992 / Gerald Gardner.
p.   cm.
ISBN 0-517-08240-3 : $4.99
1. Presidents—United States—Election—1992—Caricatures and
cartoons.   2. United States—Politics and government—1989—
Caricatures and cartoons.   3. American wit and humor, Pictorial.
I. Title
E884.G37   1992   92-16795
973.928′0207—dc20   CIP

8 7 6 5 4 3 2 1

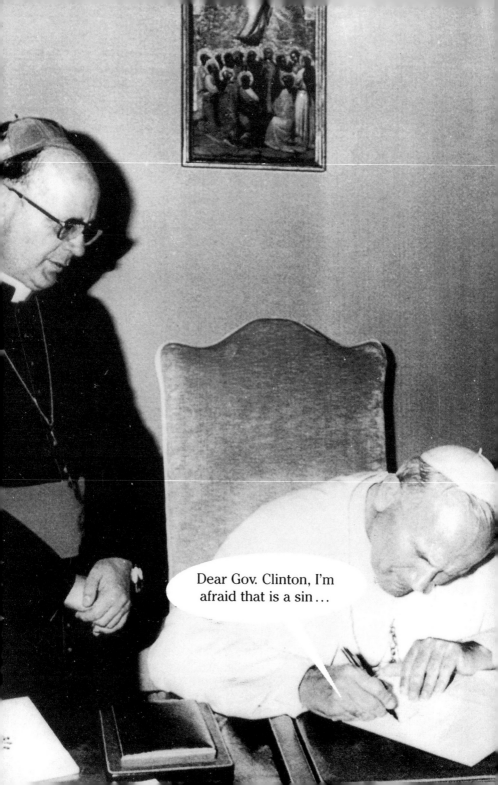

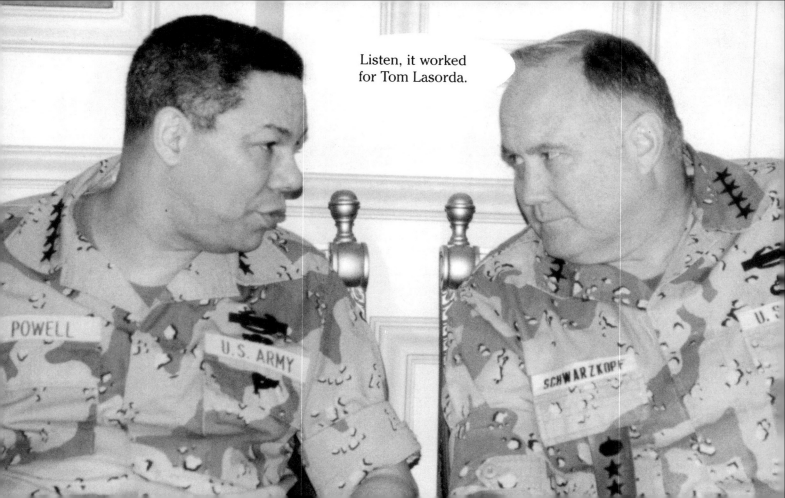

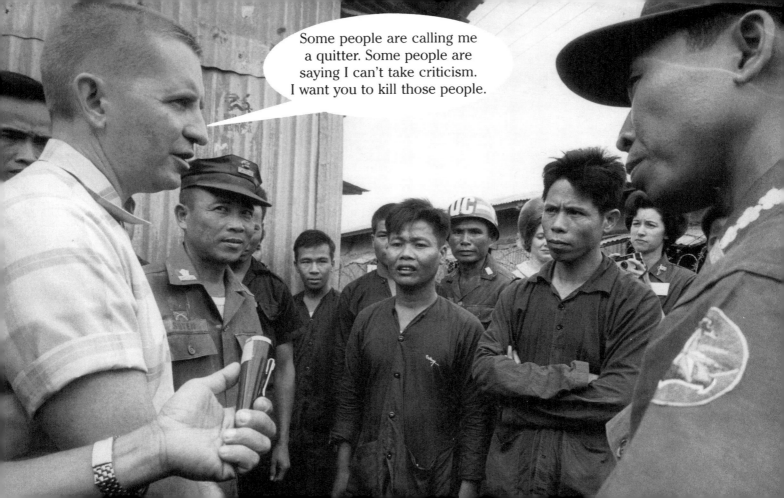